AMERICA'S FAVORITE SYMBOLS

THE STATUE OF LIBERTY
SYMBOL OF FREEDOM

JINNOW KHALID

New York

Published in 2021 by The Rosen Publishing Group, Inc.
29 East 21st Street, New York, NY 10010

Portion of this work were originally authored by Walter LaPlante and published as *The Statue of Liberty*. All new material in this edition authored by Jinnow Khalid.

Editor: Elizabeth Krajnik
Book Design: Reann Nye

Photo Credits: Cover, p.1 xo.xo_mandy/Shutterstock.com; Series Art sunwart/Shutterstock.com; p. 5 spyarm/Shutterstock.com; p. 6 https://commons.wikimedia.org/wiki/File:Abraham_Lincoln_half_length_seatet,_April_10,_1865.jpg; p. 7 https://commons.wikimedia.org/wiki/File:Édouard_René_de_Laboulaye_by_Nadar.jpg; p. 9 Alinari Archives/Alinari/Getty Images; p. 11 ullstein bild Dtl./ullstein bild/Getty Images; p. 13 Courtesy of the Library of Congress; p. 15 Universal History Archive/Universal Images Group/Getty Images; p. 17 Felix Lipov/Shutterstock.com; p. 19 UbjsP/Shutterstock.com; p. 21 TIMOTHY A. CLARY/AFP/Getty Images.

Library of Congress Cataloging-in-Publication Data

Names: Khalid, Jinnow, author.
Title: The statue of liberty : symbol of freedom / Jinnow Khalid.
Description: New York : PowerKids Press, [2021] | Series: America's favorite symbols | Includes index.
Identifiers: LCCN 2019050282 | ISBN 9781725317352 (paperback) | ISBN 9781725317376 (library binding) | ISBN 9781725317369 (6 pack)
Subjects: LCSH: Statue of Liberty (New York, N.Y.)–History–Juvenile literature. | New York (N.Y.)–Buildings, structures, etc.–Juvenile literature.
Classification: LCC F128.64.L6 K49 2021 | DDC 974.7/1–dc23
LC record available at https://lccn.loc.gov/2019050282

Manufactured in the United States of America

CPSIA Compliance Information: Batch #CSPK20. For Further Information contact Rosen Publishing, New York, New York at 1-800-237-9932.

CONTENTS

Symbol of American Pride

Since 1886, the Statue of Liberty has welcomed people from all over the world. Liberty means freedom. For many **immigrants**, coming to the United States means being free. Today, the Statue of Liberty is a **symbol** of American pride.

A Gift from France

France and the United States worked together during the **American Revolution**. In 1865, a man named Édouard-René de Laboulaye said that France should give the United States a gift to honor freedom and **democracy**. The gift would also honor Abraham Lincoln's work as president.

Abraham Lincoln

Édouard-René de Laboulaye

A Giant Statue

Laboulaye chose French **sculptor** Frédéric-Auguste Bartholdi to create the gift, which would be a giant statue. In 1870, Bartholdi began making plans for the statue, to be called Liberty **Enlightening** the World. Bartholdi chose Bedloe's Island in New York Harbor as the site for the statue.

Bartholdi's plan was for a statue of a woman wearing a crown and a robe, or a long, loose piece of clothing. She would be holding a torch, or a flaming light usually carried in the hand, and a **tablet**. Work on the statue began in France in 1876.

Working on the Statue

Work on the pedestal, or base, started in 1884 in the United States. Workers took the statue apart and shipped it from France to the United States by boat. The statue arrived on June 17, 1885. Then, workers put the statue back together on top of the pedestal.

Dedicating the Statue

President Grover Cleveland **dedicated** the statue on October 28, 1886. Thousands of people showed up to see the statue's face, which had been veiled, or covered, by the French flag. Fireworks and a parade followed the dedication.

Statue Facts

From the feet to the tip of the torch, the Statue of Liberty stands almost 152 feet (46.3 m) tall. The inside of the statue is made of iron. The outside is covered in thin sheets of copper, which is the same metal that pennies are made of.

Statue Symbols

The Statue of Liberty's torch is a symbol of enlightenment. It's meant to show us the way to liberty. Her tablet is a symbol of the law. It has the date of American **independence**—July 4, 1776—on it.

Visiting the Statue of Liberty

Every year, around 4 million people visit the Statue of Liberty. To get to Liberty Island, you have to take a boat. Then, you can visit the grounds, go inside the pedestal, and even climb up the 377 steps to the crown!

Timeline

1865
Édouard-René de Laboulaye says that France should give the United States a gift.

1870
Frédéric-Auguste Bartholdi begins making plans for the Statue of Liberty.

1876
Work on the statue begins in France.

1884
Work on the statue base begins in the United States.

June 17, 1885
The parts of the Statue of Liberty arrive in the United States.

1886
Work on the pedestal is completed.

October 28, 1886
President Grover Cleveland dedicates the Statue of Liberty.

GLOSSARY

American Revolution: The war of 1775–1783 in which 13 British colonies in North America broke free from British rule and became the United States of America.

dedicate: To open to public use.

democracy: A government elected by the people, directly or indirectly.

enlighten: To give knowledge or understanding to someone.

immigrant: A person who comes to a country to live there.

independence: Freedom from outside control or support.

sculptor: A person who makes sculptures, or pieces of art that are made by carving or molding clay, stone, metal, etc.

symbol: Something that stands for something else.

tablet: A flat piece of stone, clay, or wood that has writing on it.

INDEX

WEBSITES

Due to the changing nature of Internet links, PowerKids Press has developed an online list of websites related to the subject of this book. This site is updated regularly. Please use this link to access the list: www.powerkidslinks.com/afs/statue